Decorative Floors

in a weekend

Decorative Floors

in a weekend

Catherine Cumming

BETTERWAY BOOKS

CINCINNATI, OHIO

Introduction

For most of us, the idea of new flooring is a daunting thought involving a major upheaval and great expense! I hope that this book will show you otherwise—that creating your own floor design can be a lot of fun and very rewarding. With planning and preparation, these projects can easily be completed over a weekend and many cost no more than the price of a can of paint and some floor varnish.

One of the great advantages of these varnished finishes is that, unlike wall-to-wall carpet, you can spill almost anything on them (even red wine!) and mop it up without a trace. They are easy to maintain, easy to clean, and easy to change or repaint. Why not rip up that old carpet, take it to your local dump, and make a fresh start?

If you have a wooden floor, and you would like to retain and renovate it, I show you various options for staining, sealing, waxing, etc., and help you choose the most suitable finish for the room you have in mind. You might want to keep the look of wood and create a limed effect, or choose a color wash that will highlight the natural grain.

If your floorboards are beyond repair and require too much in the way of filling and replacing, for example, then painting might be the best option. If you are left with an uneven and lumpy surface, you could choose a distressed effect that would actually be improved by this. Or, you could woodgrain. This would cover any repairs, and an uneven surface would just add to the look of a solid, mellow wood.

Or why not lay new sheets of hardboard down and start with a clean canvas?

You could paint a formal tiled pattern, a compass, or even simulate a more opulent finish such as marble or old flagstones. You may opt for a stenciled look, a Matisse-style cutout, or a bright and colorful runner for the stairs. The projects vary in style, so I am sure that there is something for most people to choose from. And remember—all these projects can be painted in many different colors and styles. So there is really no excuse for not trying them out!

Most of the techniques described here are really only possible due to the recent availability of new improved paint products. Water-based acrylic products such as floor paint, tile primer, and special floor varnish are nontoxic, fast drying, and very tough. The painted tile project is a good example of their use—now even cracked tiles can be mended and painted in any number of ways.

For some projects you may wish to invest in a few special tools and brushes, such as nippers for cutting mosaic tiles, woodgraining combs, or a softener brush for painting marble, but in most cases normal household paintbrushes will be all that you need. It is, however, very worthwhile to invest in a pair of knee pads. These are soft pads that you strap to your legs to make the floor feel like a cushion, and certainly make the work much more comfortable.

Do not overlook the importance of your floor—its style and design can determine the whole nature of a room. The most important factor of all, though, is to enjoy it, to have fun with it, and to have only happy memories when you look down at your feet!

An important note on preparation

Preparation for all decorating is extremely important. With floors it is essential that the correct paints, primers, and sealers are used together and adhere well. When buying paint and primer check the labels to be sure that they are suitable to use together. There is no point in applying a tough top coat of floor varnish if the paint underneath has not stuck to the primer—it is at this point (of least adhesion) that the paint will chip. Make sure that the products you use are suitable at every stage.

A few of the projects in this book use latex paints, usually because of the quick drying times, the nontoxic qualities, and the range of colors available. You cannot, however, use latex paint if the floorboards you are painting already have an eggshell base or a varnish. The best paint to use on eggshell paint would be another eggshell. With a varnished floor, you would have to sand off the varnish completely, prime, and then coat with matte latex. This is very time consuming and best to avoid completely. Instead, you could sand down the varnish so that an eggshell paint or another solvent-based paint can then bind onto this and adhere well. The importance of checking every product you use cannot be stressed enough. Always ask in the paint store or even check with the manufacturer if you are not sure about any particular product.

The same is true for final floor varnish. Water-based acrylic finishes can take both acrylic and oil-based varnish, but solvent-based varnishes must be used on solvent-based paint (such as oil-based eggshell). For most of the projects in this book, we have used acrylic-based fast-drying products.

Finally, before you start painting, preparing, or varnishing any floor, make sure you have a clean, dust-free room. Before you start, vacuum and then wipe the floor thoroughly with a tack cloth. Use a tack cloth at every stage to ensure a dust-free finish.

Color wash in two colors

These bare wooden floorboards are gently color washed with thin, transparent layers of diluted latex paint, which seep into the wood, allowing the grain and texture to show.

Color washing is a simple technique to use on bare wood and the effect can be as light or as heavy as you wish—just add more or less water to the mixture. Ready-mixed wood stains can also be used for this effect and these tend to sink more deeply into the grain of the wood.

A particular advantage of latex paint is that, unlike wood stain, there are hundreds of colors to choose from. It is also possible to blend in thicker versions of the latex wash to cover certain areas more opaquely, and so disguise knots or any repairs in the wood.

To add a simple pattern to a floor as shown here, simply mask off square shapes of various sizes on the color-washed base and wash over a second time in another color. The base color affects the color of the second wash and shows through a little underneath, so for this reason it is easier to paint a dark color on top of a lighter base.

You can, of course, use any shape or pattern, either across the floor as I have or as a border. Diluted latex paint dries very quickly, so if you are color washing your floor on a warm summer's weekend with the windows open, you will probably have it finished with plenty of time to spare.

Refurbishing old floorboards

Lifting up the carpet and exposing your old floorboards for the first time need not be such a daunting task and can be quite a discovery with the potential for some interesting effects!

Planning your time

DAY ONE
AM: Sand the floor with electric sander

PM: Sand edges, apply putty, and prepare floor for staining

DAY TWO
AM: Apply wood stain

PM: Apply wax, then buff; or apply floor sealer; or apply floor varnish

Tools and materials

Tool rental: electric sander and edger, and sandpaper for both

Wood putty and knife

Small strips of wood to fill gaps between floorboards

Tack cloth and lint-free cloth

Fine-grit sandpaper

Wood stain (if applicable), latex gloves, and sponge or brush

Floor wax (if applicable)

Floor sealer (if applicable)

Floor varnish (if applicable)

Buffer for wax (if applicable)

Wax filler sticks (if applicable)

Household paintbrushes

It is possible just to clean old floorboards—proprietary cleaners will remove old varnish and wax and a new top finish can be applied. In order to accept a new wood stain, however, old floorboards must be properly sanded. Plan ahead for this weekend and reserve your floor sander in advance—there is quite a demand for weekend rental.

There are many different ways of finishing a wooden floor—I have picked four different finishes to demonstrate on page 13.

One method is to apply wax directly on bare wood (*opposite, top right*); this finish is suitable for an area that does not get too much wear. Wax is a unique and beautiful finish, but needs maintaining. Re-buff the floor occasionally when it is looking dull, and if no shine appears, it is probably time for a new coat of wax. How often you need to reapply this will depend on how much wear the floor gets. Wax is also stained by water and can be slippery, so it is not a practical choice if you have children or pets!

Another method shows floorboards stained with antique pine finished with wax on top of a sealer (*opposite, top left*). This effect is more durable than wax alone but still requires regular applications and polishing. On small areas, a small drill attachment is sufficient for buffing liquid wax, but for larger areas, rent an electric buffer.

A third option, shown here with a dark walnut-colored stain, is simply to seal the wood (*opposite, bottom right*). This is the most durable finish. It is totally waterproof, and with a matte finish, the surface will not be slippery.

Finally, I have shown floorboards stained white and finished with a gloss varnish (*opposite, bottom left*). A few coats of varnish may be required—especially on old, dry wood. This surface is durable and waterproof. In time, when the varnish starts to wear off, it can be sanded down and reapplied.

Wood stains are now available in lots of colors. I applied the stain in a straightforward way, but if you have more time over another weekend you could try staining with more than one color and even create an inlaid pattern. (See Color washing on page 8.)

Day One

Step 1
When renting a sanding machine make sure you are shown how to use your particular machine before you leave the store. Check the floor first for loose nails. Sand the floor using a coarse-grit sandpaper first, gradually working down to medium-grit, and finishing with fine-grit.

Step 2
Use an edging sander to reach the corners and edges of the floor up to the baseboard. Again, start with a coarse-grit paper and work down to a fine-grit one.

Step 3
Apply wood putty with a putty knife. Choose a color as close as possible to the desired finish. Putty will not accept dye in the same way as the wood, so when filling the hole try not to go over the edge since this will show through the stain. Let it dry for about 15 minutes, then sand down.

Step 4
Wet the floor and lightly sand. This will keep the grain from swelling and raising once a water-based stain is applied.

Step 5
Use a tack cloth to remove any remaining dust before applying a dye or any finish.

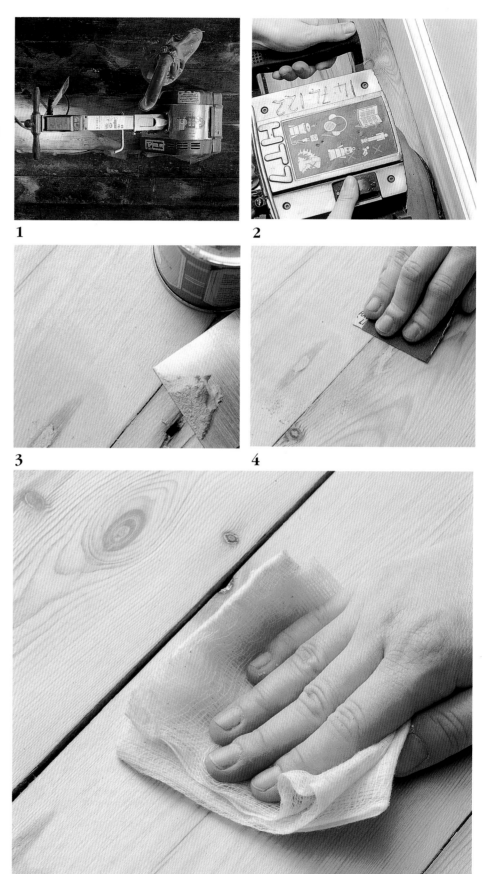

1

2

3

4

5

6

Day Two

Step 6

Apply wood stain with a sponge applicator or a brush. Test the color first on an identical piece of wood.

Step 7

Wipe with a lint-free cloth. I used an old sheet. Apply a second coat of stain if required.

Now, to finish a stain and enhance the grain of the wood, there are various options: applying floor sealer (Steps 8 and 9); applying a varnish (Step 10); or applying a liquid floor wax (Steps 11, 12, 13, and 14)

Applying floor sealer

Step 8

Apply floor sealer with a brush. Always check the manufacturer's instructions— different products require different applications. This is a very tough matte finish. It is long-wearing and is not slippery, unlike wax and varnish.

Step 9

Leave for a few minutes, then wipe off the excess sealer with a cloth. The next evening apply a second coat of sealer, and an additional one if required once this is dry. Check the drying times recommended by the manufacturer.

7

8

9

Checking old floorboards

Before sanding down old floorboards check for loose nails and make sure they are hammered back down. Saw some small strips of wood to fill any gaps between the boards, push them in place, then sand them in with the floorboards.

Applying a varnish

Step 10

Apply floor varnish with a brush. Most varnishes come in three different finishes—matte, satin, and gloss. The next evening apply a second coat of varnish, and another one if required once this is dry. Check the drying times recommended by the manufacturer.

Applying a liquid floor wax

Step 11

Apply liquid floor wax with a brush, painting it on the floorboards in the direction of the woodgrain.

10

Getting rid of sanding dust

After sanding the floor, it is best not to broom clean but to use a vacuum cleaner to remove the dust.

11

12

Step 12

When the wax is dry (in about half an hour) buff the surface. For large areas rent a buffing machine. For smaller areas use a drill brush.

Step 13

To disguise new cracks that open up and small holes, use wax filler sticks. Choose the color closest to the finish of the wood.

Step 14

Buff the wax filler stick inserts with a cloth.

13

14

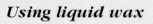

Using liquid wax

When using liquid wax be aware that it will color and yellow the wood more than a varnish or sealer will. This will be more apparent on a pale wood, so test on a scrap of identical wood before you start.

Limed-effect floorboards

Here, new pine floorboards have been treated with a limed, or pickled, effect and the overall finish is a soft, hazy look that complements cool, neutral furnishings.

Planning your time

DAY ONE
AM: Apply shellac; color wash (or stain) wood

PM: Apply sanding sealer—this dries quickly; start opening up grain with a wire brush

DAY TWO
AM: Prepare and apply paste

PM: Apply and wipe off paste; seal with tough acrylic floor varnish

Tools and materials

White shellac

Latex paint for color wash or wood stain

Sanding sealer

White latex paint

Plaster of Paris

Bucket

Wire brush

Cloth

Large paintbrush

Tough acrylic floor varnish

Three hundred or so years ago liming paste was prepared as an extremely toxic solution that was applied to kill off the woodworm and bugs that were eating their way through wooden buildings. This gray-white paste also enhanced the color and grain of the wood; the look later became fashionable and a less lethal substance was produced purely for decoration.

Liming is traditionally, and more often, applied to an open-grained wood such as oak (the liming paste needs to be pushed into the grain of the wood, so the open pores of oak grain are ideal for

this type of floor finish). However, in this project I have used close-grained pine wood, and the pores of the grain therefore have to be opened by vigorous brushing with a hard wire brush. For the actual liming, I have used a simple homemade paste. Ready-made liming waxes are available, but they cannot be sealed and are therefore not suitable for floors. The water-based paste I have used can be sealed with a tough acrylic floor varnish.

For this project, floorboards should be either new or completely free of wax and varnish. I first color washed new pine floorboards in gray, but you could also use a wood stain. Most dull colors would be a suitable base, since this brings more definition to the white limed recesses and adds to the soft and mellow look of liming.

1

Day One

Step 1
Apply shellac (if wood is new).

Step 2
Color wash the boards first for a soft base color. Apply a gray latex wash (see Color washing on page 8) and allow to dry.

Step 3
Apply a coat of quick-drying sanding sealer. Sanding sealer is actually designed to fill the grain before sanding, but in this case it seals the wood before opening the grain with a wire brush.

Step 4
Open up the grain (or in this case color-washed base) with a wire brush. Brush vigorously but carefully, being sure to move the brush only in the direction of the grain—any marks going across the grain will show up once the paste is applied.

2

3

4

Keeping a dark base

When wire brushing your base color, you may find that too much color is lifted off and you would prefer to keep a much darker base color. An alternative method is to wire brush the bare wood as the second step after shellacking. Apply your dark base coat and then seal this with white French polish (that will not fill the grain). Then rub in the paste and continue as before. As always, test on a piece of scrap wood first.

Day Two

Step 5

Prepare the white paste in a bucket—pour the white latex paint into a bucket and add the white plaster of Paris until it is a paste-like consistency. Add water periodically when the paste becomes too thick.

Step 6

With a large paintbrush, apply a thick coat of paste, pressing it into the grain of the wood. Add more water if the paste becomes too thick.

Step 7

Using a damp cloth, wipe off the excess paste.

Step 8

Wipe again with a clean cloth.

Step 9

Finally, seal with two coats of acrylic floor varnish. This will slightly soften the white color when wet, but as the varnish dries the white will show through again.

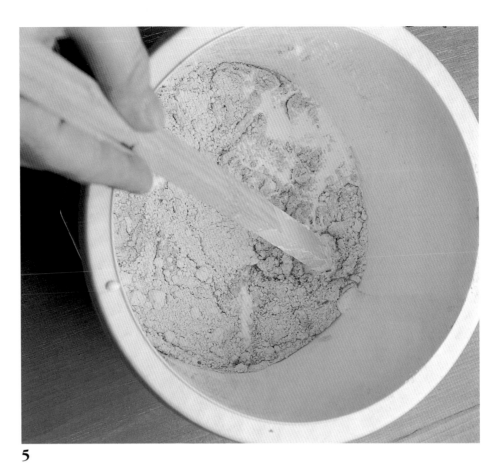

5

6

7

Avoiding a darkened effect

You can also seal with sanding sealer before applying the final varnish. This will keep the varnish from soaking in and slightly darkening the floor.

8

9

Compass in matte latex

This compass design is much easier to draw and paint than it might appear. Using household latex paint, it makes an attractive and unusual decoration.

Planning your time

DAY ONE
AM: Mark off the compass shape in chalk

PM: Paint in the two top colors of the compass

DAY TWO
AM: Paint in lettering

PM: Seal with two coats of tough acrylic floor varnish

Tools and materials

2½ quarts of latex paint for the base color

1 quart each of two latex colors for the compass

Ruler

Chalk

Household paintbrush

Small brush for corners and lettering

Transfer paper

Pencil

Tough acrylic floor varnish

Clean paint roller for varnish

D espite the wide selection of fast-drying floor paints, latex paint is still an interesting option. Its main advantage is its drying time—in warm weather two coats can easily be applied in a day. By preparing the base coat the night or day before, you will find that this project will leave you plenty of time for a long lunch on both days!

There are hundreds of ready-made colors to choose from—and since only small quantities of latex paint are needed for the compass, you can mix small amounts exactly.

However you select your colors, it is always helpful to establish all three colors before you start. Try them out on paper, but remember that they dry slightly differently, so wait until they are dry (or dry them quickly with a hair dryer) before you finally decide.

With correct preparation and a tough acrylic floor varnish, this is a durable finish. The star shape of the compass is often used in floor patterns and is quite easy to draw. There are many variations to try out in all sorts of shapes, colors, and languages!

Prepare the base coat of latex paint the night before you intend to paint the compass.

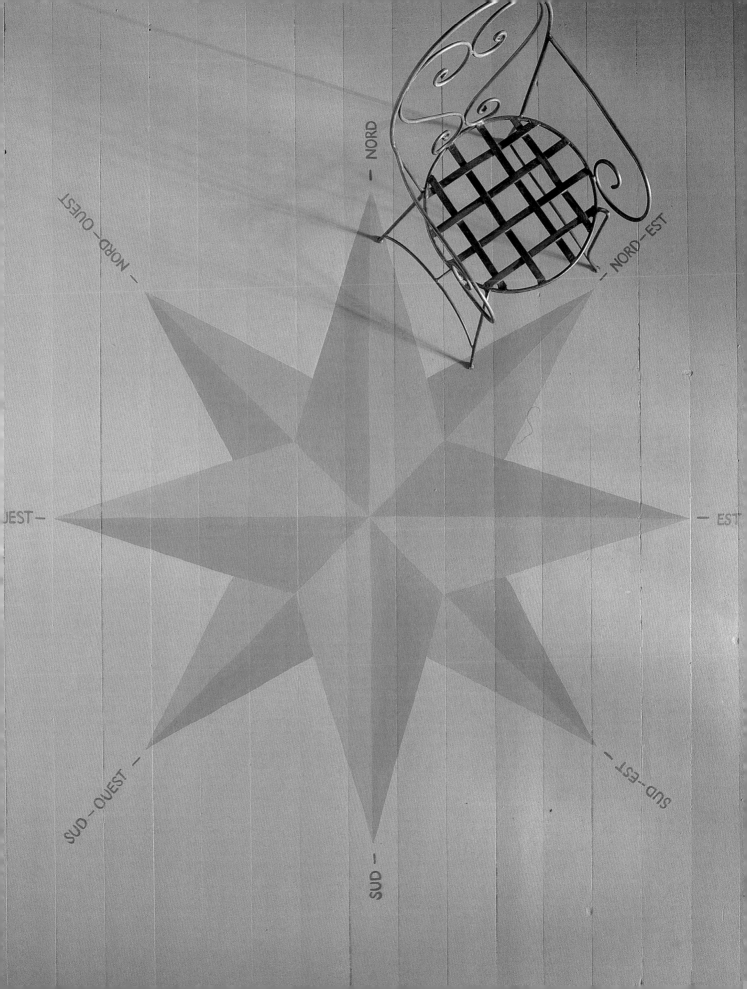

1

2

3

Day One

Step 1

Measure and mark out your design on the floor that already has a latex base coat. First, draw a cross, then an "X" shape over this to make an eight-pointed star.

Step 2

To complete the star shape, measure along the cross one-third from the inside and mark a square along these end points. Join the corners of the squares to the tips of the cross to form the larger points of the compass. Then join the four smaller points to the midpoints of the square to complete an eight-pointed star shape.

Step 3

Fill in the gray areas first, using a household paintbrush.

Step 4

Use a small brush to reach into the corners.

4

Using nonlatex paint

This project used matte latex paint. Because it dries quickly, two coats can be applied over a short time. You could, however, also use acrylic floor paint, or eggshell, or even gloss paint. But remember that an oil-based paint needs a solvent-based floor varnish or sealer. (See note on preparation page 7.)

5

6

7

Step 5
Fill in the dark blue areas in the same way as in Step 3.

Step 6
Use transfer paper to copy an even outline for the lettering. (I first typed out the words, then photocopied and enlarged them to the correct size.)

Day Two

Step 7
Fill in the lettering with a thin brush.

Step 8
When the paint is completely dry, protect the design with two coats of acrylic floor varnish. I used a roller for quick coverage.

8

Medieval tile pattern in acrylic floor paint

With the new acrylic floor paints you can give free rein to your imagination. The pattern used here is based on the floor tile design in a medieval church.

For years floor paint was only available in two or three colors. Oil based, it was very smelly and took a long time to dry properly.

Fast-drying acrylic floor paint has now changed all that. It really is quick drying, it does not smell, and is now available in a much more exciting range of colors.

I have used this paint on primed hardboard here and created a formal pattern with just three colors. You could make this project as simple or as complex as you choose. Color combinations and patterns are endless and there are many source books available to help you.

As this paint is especially formulated for floors, no sealer or varnish is needed. If you should ever wish to change your design or color scheme, just lightly sand down the surface and simply repaint it.

The night before you start this project, or even earlier, paint a base coat of gray acrylic floor paint on the floor.

Laying hardboard

Hardboard is laid by butting up large sheets together and securing them, smooth side up, with staples. Start laying the boards from the center of the room, and cut the outer ones to size. Buy a manual staple gun and mallet to secure the boards to the floor. You can rent electric staple guns, but they are harder to control. The mallet method is best and not as difficult as it looks.

Once new hardboard has been laid, fill any holes, then apply primer paint, and when it is dry, paint on your base color.

Thin particle board is also a suitable material; this is more expensive than hardboard, but is sturdier. Both materials have an equally good smooth surface.

Planning your time

DAY ONE
AM: Plan the design on graph paper and mark out the floor

PM: Paint the red sections of the floor

DAY TWO
AM: Paint the green sections

PM: Paint the triangles and go over the areas that need a second coat

Tools and materials

Acrylic floor paint in your chosen three colors

Household paintbrush

Small brush for corners and triangles

Chalk

Straightedge or chalk string

Tape measure or measuring stick

Damp cloth

Roller and tray for applying base coat

Day One

Step 1
Prepare the floor with a base coat of gray acrylic floor paint and let this dry thoroughly overnight.

Step 2
Draw your plan on graph paper first to see how the pattern will fit into the shape of your room. Mark the center of the room and start the pattern from this point.

Step 3
Measure equal squares over the entire floor.

Step 4
Use a long straightedge to mark these squares off with chalk.

Step 5
Cut out a square template to mark the smaller squares within some of the larger ones.

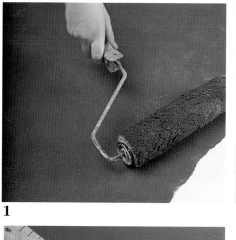

1

2

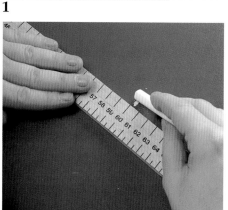

3

4

5

Alternative chalking method of marking

Another method of marking the chalk lines is to rub some chalk along a piece of string. Tack it down at both ends of the floor, or ask some helpers to hold it at both ends while you snap it to the floor, marking a straight line.

6

Step 6

So as not to get confused later, mark which sections are to be painted red, and which green.

Step 7

Fill in the red sections with a household paintbrush. Start in the middle of the floor and work outward.

Day Two

Step 8

Once the red paint is dry, paint the green sections.

Step 9

Mark off the triangle shapes—green ones around the small red squares, red ones around the small green squares.

Step 10

Paint the insides of the triangles.

Step 11

Once all the paint is dry, wipe off the chalk marks with a damp cloth. Acrylic floor paint is durable and does not require varnishing.

Where to start painting

Remember to start painting at the center or back of the room—do not paint yourself into a corner!

7

8

9

10

11

Greek key stencil border

Stencils have been used in decoration for hundreds of years and by many cultures. Here is a simple, cost-efficient technique for achieving an even and regular pattern.

Planning your time

DAY ONE
AM: Apply beeswax to the floor; design and cut your stencil

PM: Stencil on one section of the key shape and one section of the gold check

DAY TWO
AM: Reverse stencil and paint in the second part of the key area and second gold check

PM: Paint in details such as the gold line with fast-drying gold paint; chip off wax and lightly distress

Tools and materials

Acrylic floor paint for base coat and roller to apply this

Artist's acrylic paints and gold paint in two different tones

Chalk and measuring stick

Graph paper and acetate sheets

Craft knife

Beeswax cream

Spray adhesive and stencil brushes

Fine-grit sandpaper and paint scraper

This stencil was taken from an ancient Greek key pattern. It was made out of thick acetate sheets that were easy to see through and match up with the second part of this two-part design. Suitable alternatives are manila card (a special oiled stencil card) or any thin cardboard you could prepare yourself with a coat of varnish. Paper can be used for speed for very small areas, but will not last very long.

You could make up your own stencil design, or copy and adapt a pattern you have seen, or even use photocopies of existing designs enlarged or reduced to fit your own floor.

If you are new to stenciling, it may be best to stencil onto a nonporous base coat such as acrylic eggshell; this will enable you to wipe off any mistakes or leaks. If your base coat is porous, such as a color-washed floor, you could varnish this first before stenciling. Because of the distressed look of this particular stencil design, I have not worried too much about paint adhesion— more wear and tear actually adds to the effect.

Ready-made stencils can now be bought at many craft stores and home-improvement centers. This saves time, but limits your subject matter and the scale of the design and will, of course, considerably detract from the enjoyment of making your very own and unique floor border!

The night before starting this project paint the floor with a base coat of acrylic floor paint; two coats will probably be required.

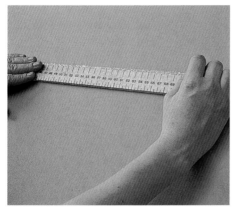

1

Day One

Step 1

Using chalk, mark off the floor where you would like the border to run, and how large you would like the pattern to be. Start from the corners and measure the length of the floor, making sure the pattern will fit approximately along this area. Small discrepancies can be improved later with a link piece (see Step 12).

Step 2

Draw your design on graph paper. (Or, alternately, prepare a photocopy.)

Step 3

Lay a sheet of thick acetate over the design and trace the design onto the acetate with a pencil.

2

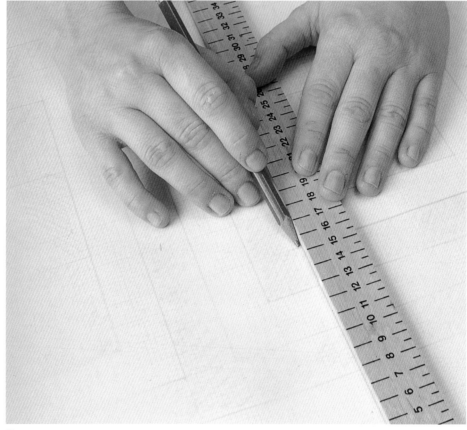

3

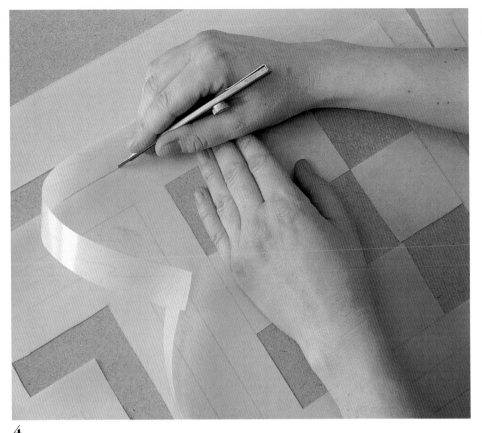

4

Step 4

Using a craft knife, cut out one side of the key design only and the outer corner squares and central square of the checked section.

Step 5

For the remaining squares on the check, make up a separate stencil, but leave a tiny link joining the center square to the corner ones.

Step 6

Apply beeswax cream here and there to the floor where the stencil is to be applied and allow this to dry. It will be chipped off once the stencil has been painted on over the wax and has dried; this will help to create a distressed look within the stencil pattern. Apply the cream unevenly and with lumps so that the effect will look as natural as possible.

Step 7

It is possible to position the stencil with tape. I used spray adhesive since it fixes the stencil more evenly and can be stuck down and lifted off a number of times before having to reapply the adhesive.

Step 8

Prepare the acrylic colors you are going to use (I used a piece of painted hardboard as a palette). Dab the brush onto the paint and then onto a board or a cloth to remove excess paint from the brush.

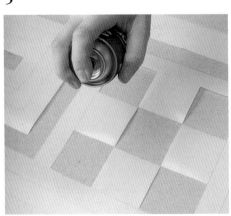

5

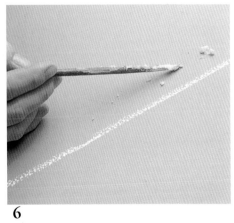

6

7

8

9

Step 9

Starting from the corner, stencil on the first part of the key shape and the checked pattern.

Day Two

Step 10

Once the paint is completely dry, turn the stencil around and stencil on the second part of the pattern—that is, the reverse key pattern.

Step 11

Use the separate stencil to stencil on the second gold color of the checked square.

10

11

Choosing acetate and paints

Do not use thin, clear acetate to make stencils because it tears too easily. I used artist's acrylic paint to stencil with, but special stencil paint and other paints can also be used.

12

13

14

Step 12
If the stencil does not fit exactly along the length of the floor, a linking piece can be cut to solve this. Measure the gap and design the link piece accordingly.

Step 13
Paint in any details by hand, marking them off with chalk first as a guideline.

Step 14
Once the paint is dry, gently chip off the beeswax with a putty knife or a paint scraper.

Step 15
Sand with a fine-grit paper to create a worn, distressed look. As this is a distressed pattern and has been painted on a tough acrylic floor paint, I chose not to varnish it but to leave it to distress further. If it starts to wear away too much, it can then be sealed.

15

Marble tile effect

This project shows you how to reproduce a marble effect and transform a base of hardboard into a rich and opulent surface with depth and color.

For many centuries the beauty and richness of natural marble has been imitated. Sometimes it is simulated to perfection, sometimes painted as an effect. We have opted for painting tiles of richly colored stone-like marble in a checkerboard effect.

The smooth surface of hardboard is perfect as a base to work on (see page 26 for how to lay hardboard), but you will need to apply a coat of primer paint first and then paint it with a smooth base coat of acrylic eggshell. For this project I applied two coats of acrylic eggshell paint as a base, choosing a sandy brown color because of the strong, warm colors of this particular marble effect.

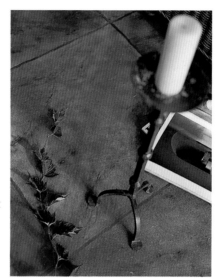

There are all kinds of possibilities, not only for color, but also for creating inlaid patterns with marbling. Remember, though, to keep the sections fairly small as acrylic paints have to be worked quickly—if the glaze starts to dry it becomes difficult to soften. It is best to work on sections no bigger than a 20" (50cm) square.

This project is probably the most demanding in the book, but once you get into the swing of the technique, it is extremely enjoyable. Try experimenting with different shapes and colors. If in doubt, look at real marble and stone for inspiration—without exception it is always beautiful!

Planning your time

DAY ONE
AM: Mark out floor and start painting red marble sections

PM: Continue painting red marble squares

DAY TWO
AM: Paint orange marble squares

PM: You may finish the orange squares in the morning or may want to carry on in the afternoon

Tools and materials

Acrylic eggshell base coat and roller to apply it

Acrylic glaze

Artist's acrylic colors (Mars violet and burnt umber for red sections, and burnt sienna and burnt umber for orange sections)

Tough acrylic floor sealer

Household paintbrush

Sturdy feather such as a goose feather (use a naturally shed feather or buy from a craft store)

Softening brush (or soft dusting brush)

Cloth

Thin brush for painting grout line if preferred

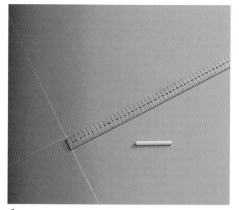

1

2

3

Day One

Step 1
Make sure that the acrylic eggshell base coat applied the night before is completely dry, then measure and mark off large squares across the whole floor.

Step 2
Apply a coat of clear acrylic glaze over one complete square.

Step 3
Dab acrylic color (Mars violet) straight from the tube onto the tip of the brush.

Step 4
Apply the paint, pressing the brush firmly into the glaze to avoid harsh streaks of color.

4

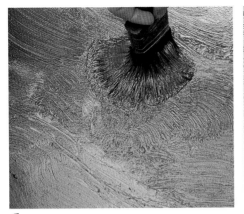

5

6

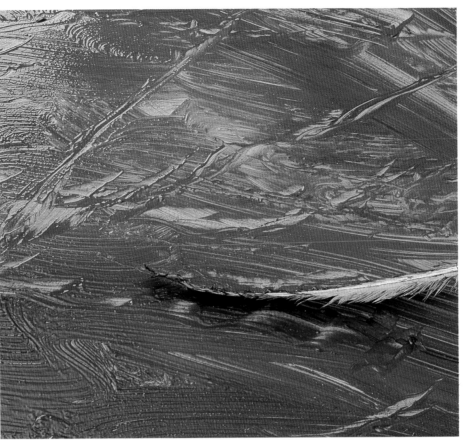

7

Step 5
Apply a second color (burnt umber)
in the same way, blending this through
the existing Mars violet.

Step 6
Apply some burnt umber acrylic along
the edge of a feather.

Step 7
Mark in the veins of the marble,
keeping to one direction.

Step 8
Dab this glaze with a cotton cloth
(I used a torn-up old cotton bedsheet)
in the direction of the veining, turning
it now and then to keep it fairly clean.
Discard the cloth and use another one
if it becomes too wet with paint.

8

9

Step 9

Soften very gently with a soft brush
(I used a dusting brush), using only
the tips of the brush to blend the
colors. Wipe the softener brush now
and then with a cloth to keep the
bristles clean and dry. If the brush
becomes clogged, wash it with soapy
water and dry it thoroughly with a hair
dryer before you continue.

Step 10

Add more veins if required and soften
again. This has to be done quickly—
before the glaze dries too much.

Step 11

Open up any very dark veins with the
clean tip of a feather.

10

11

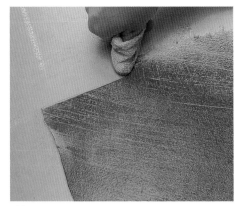

12

Step 12

Wipe off the edges of the squares with a damp cloth, leaving a clean edge. Allow to dry. You could also apply floor sealer to the red squares and allow these to dry overnight before painting neighboring squares if you wish.

Day Two

Step 13

When the red squares are completely dry, paint in the orange squares in the same way. Carefully wipe off any glaze overlapping onto the red squares. Paint in grout lines, or leave natural joints.

Step 14

When the paint is dry, varnish the entire floor with tough acrylic floor sealer, or just varnish the orange squares if you have already done the red ones. You could use a gloss, matte, or satin finish. I prefer a satin finish as it looks softer than gloss; a slight sheen gives the marble a little more depth than a flat matte finish. On the following day apply, another coat to seal the whole floor.

Fine marbling

For fine marbling, use very soft, special softening brushes. For the effect here I used a soft dusting brush, which was cheaper than a softening brush.

13

14

Découpage

Découpage allows you the freedom to turn your floor into a giant picture, creating themed images or abstract shapes. Here the work of the artist Matisse has provided inspiration.

Records of découpage date back to the seventeenth century, when engraved and printed designs were cut out of paper and mounted onto furniture that was varnished and finished so that the cutouts appeared to be hand painted. The craft later became a popular pastime in England during the nineteenth century.

For this project, I have moved away from the traditional use of découpage and paid homage to the French artist Henri Matisse (1869-1954) and the work that he produced with cutouts. Matisse cut out his shapes from sheets of paper colored with gouache, then pasted them onto a support.

I have cut aquatic shapes out of white paper and glued them onto the floor in the style of his picture *Oceania the Sky*. I do not think Matisse would really mind this being done since adapting parts of a picture that is so beautiful makes you enjoy and appreciate it even more.

Sources for inspiration are endless—you could try cutting out wrapping paper designs, pictures in magazines, or printed cards, photocopying the designs and then enlarging or reducing them as you wish. Keep a collection of odd pieces that you like and might inspire you—you never know when or how you might use them.

Once the cutouts have been pasted down, apply two coats of floor varnish to ensure a long-wearing and protective surface.

1

Day One

Step 1
The inspiration for this design was taken from Matisse's *Oceania the Sky*. Prepare the floor with a base color; I used two coats of acrylic floor paint. While the first coat is drying, start working on the paper cutouts.

Step 2
Draw the shapes on paper.

Step 3
Cut out the shapes—the sharper your scissors, the easier this will be. Use a craft knife for corners that are difficult to reach.

Step 4
When you have cut out all the shapes, apply the second base coat of color to the floor, checking that the first is thoroughly dry.

2

3

4

Choosing paper for cutouts

Thin paper will stick to the floor and "lose itself" into the surface more easily than thick paper. Use a smooth paper that will stick evenly.

5

6

7

8

Day Two

Step 5
Lay the paper shapes out on the floor and arrange the design.

Step 6
Working one at a time, spray the shapes with spray adhesive or apply glue. Make sure you spray or glue over the entire shape and do not miss any areas of the cutout.

Step 7
Paste the shapes down firmly, making sure the whole piece has adhered properly to the floor.

Step 8
Seal the whole floor with tough solvent-based floor varnish. When the floor is dry, apply a second coat for maximum protection.

Distressed and crackled paint

This "old paint" effect is great for uneven surfaces—the glaze will create a lumpy, bumpy finish and give the impression of many layers of paint hiding underneath.

Planning your time

DAY ONE

AM: Apply beeswax and apply crackle glaze

PM: Apply latex paint

DAY TWO

AM: Rub on lighter color; chip off wax and distress

PM: Seal with tough acrylic floor sealer

Tools and materials

2½ quarts of latex paint for base coat

Two different colors of latex paint for top coat and wash (1 quart of each)

Crackle glaze

Beeswax cream

Tough acrylic floor sealer

Large household paintbrush

Thin brush to apply wax

Cloth

Scouring pad

Large putty knife or paint scraper

This technique is simple to do and is a fun way to use very strong colors together. Try experimenting with unusual color combinations—even bright colors that you would not normally consider using together can create interesting effects in this way. I used latex paint to decorate these floorboards, and there is a huge range of colors to choose from.

I used a deep violet color as a base coat, with a fairly strong pink on top of this. I then softened the pink with a much paler pink wash.

You can make the effect as subtle or as strong as you like simply by altering the amount of wax you apply to the boards. You could also add more colors to the effect; just continue to layer colors on top of the base color, adding wax at each stage before you add the crackle glaze. It is helpful to do a practice run before the weekend on a scrap board—you will be amazed at the colors you eventually decide to use!

Apply a base coat of latex paint to the boards the night before you start this project. Before buying the paint, check the coverage on the label. The exact amount you will need will depend on your room size.

1

Day One

Step 1

Having applied a base coat of matte latex paint the night before, apply beeswax cream on a thin brush. Concentrate on the edges of each board that would naturally show wear first, but put some small blobs here and there on the boards. Apply the wax in lumps and unevenly; this will dry overnight.

Step 2

Apply a coat of crackle glaze over the whole floor. Paint it on unevenly, but use long brush strokes in the direction of the floorboards. This is important: the cracks will appear where you apply this glaze, and the form that they take will be determined by how you apply it. Allow the glaze to dry; it should take about two hours, depending on the temperature.

Step 3

When the crackle glaze is dry, apply pink latex paint on top of it, and let this coat dry.

2

3

Day Two

Step 4

Cracks and blisters will have appeared in the paint. Rub some diluted top color (here, a very light pink) over the surface.

Step 5

With a wide putty knife or a paint scraper, chip off the wax along the edges of the floorboards.

Step 6

Then use a wide putty knife or a paint scraper to scrape *across* the boards, chipping off the wax haphazardly.

Step 7

Use a scouring pad to rub off more paint here and there.

Step 8

If you have chipped off too much paint, paint in the base color with a thin brush. You may, of course, prefer this effect, with yet another color showing through, and decide to leave it. Finally, when it is dry, apply tough acrylic floor sealer to protect the surface.

4

5

6

Checking the suitability of boards for distressing

This technique can be used with matte latex paint only. Make sure that the base coat is suitably prepared so that the paint adheres well. This effect is not suitable for floors that have already been painted with a hard eggshell paint or a varnish.

7

8

Old flagstones effect

To lay a real old stone floor is a very specialized task and often requires expensive material—but you can enjoy the colors and impression of stone with this paint effect.

Real stone floors are usually associated with cold and drafty dwellings, but I can assure you that the painted version is much warmer and softer to walk on!

This effect is suitable for surfaces such as hardboard (see page 26 for how to lay hardboard). It does not matter if the floor surface is dented or uneven, since these imperfections will just enhance the stone-like texture.

The decoration is achieved by rubbing matte latex paints onto a stippled base. I used a dark brown and an almost-black color to rub onto a buff-colored base. You could use other stone colors—perhaps tending toward more gray, yellow, or green. You can also alter the scale and size of the flagstones to suit the particular room you are painting.

Latex paint means that this technique is fast drying and easy to apply. It is used for a kitchen floor here, but it could be used in any room. Protected with a tough water-resistant sealer, it would even be suitable for a bathroom.

Prepare the floor with a coat of primer and then a base coat of latex paint the night before (or two coats if you can).

Planning your time

DAY ONE
AM: Prepare with a second base coat of latex paint (if you could not apply two the previous evening)

PM: Mark out flagstone shapes and stipple on second base color

DAY TWO
AM: Rub on first top coat color and start the second

PM: Finish painting with second color; paint in grout line; finally, seal with tough acrylic floor varnish

Tools and materials

Latex paint for base coat and roller to apply this

Two small quantities of top color latex paint

Household paintbrush

Cloth

Thin brush to paint grout line

Chalk

Acrylic pewter-colored paint (if required)

Tough acrylic floor varnish

Day One

Step 1
On a base coat of latex paint, mark off stone shapes with chalk.

Step 2
Stipple on the second base color of latex paint—this is a vital step that will later give texture to the effect.

Day Two

Step 3
Dab the very tip of your brush into brown latex paint so that you use just the smallest amount.

Step 4
Rub the brown paint into the floor with the brush rather than painting it on.

Step 5
Wipe the paint in with a damp cloth. As you do so, the stippled texture underneath will show through.

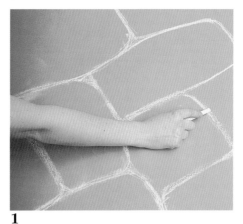

1

2

3

4

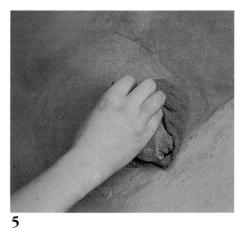

5

Step 6

Use a piece of cardboard as a mask to help keep the shading on each stone quite different.

Step 7

Apply the second color, in this case a dark gray, in the same way.

Step 8

You could also add some pewter-colored acrylic paint diluted slightly with a bit of glaze to some areas. This will give some stones a slightly metallic look.

Step 9

Paint in the grout lines using a dirty gray-brown acrylic paint applied with a thin brush.

Step 10

Shape the grout, adding darker areas within the corners that would be deeper on a real stone floor. Finally, when it is dry, seal the whole floor with a tough acrylic floor varnish.

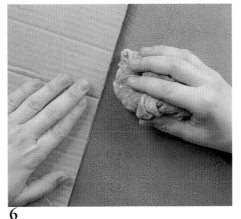

6

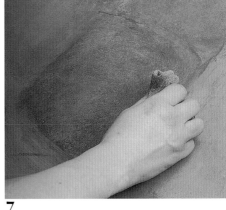

7

8

9

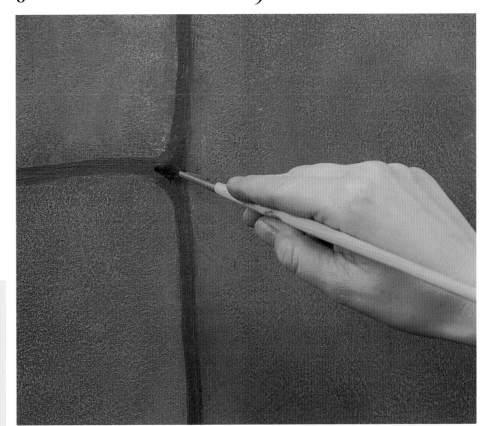

10

Stippling the flagstones

When stippling the latex base coat, do so evenly to create a natural-looking texture. Be careful not to leave too knobbly a surface since this would chip off later when the floor is walked on—keep the stippling textured, but not too prominent.

Renovating tiles with paint

Thanks to exciting new paint products, it is now possible to repair and to paint old floor tiles. A new multicolored floor can add a vibrant touch to your kitchen.

You do not have to live with patterns and colors (and cracks!) you do not like, or go to the trouble and expense of pulling up floor tiles and laying new ones. Tough and durable painted finishes can be achieved quite easily within a weekend.

There are two ways to approach the renovation of tiles. The most simple method is to use a special proprietary tile paint. The tiles should be sanded first with a fine-grit paper to provide a rough surface for the paint to stick to. Floor tiles lose their glaze through wear over time anyway, so the areas that might need more sanding are the protected areas, such as under a table or behind the door. Special tile paint is more expensive than most paint, but it is easy to use since it requires no primer and final varnish or sealer.

Another method is first to prime the tiles with a tile primer. It is then possible to use latex paint on top of this before sealing with a tough floor varnish. Eggshell and gloss paints could also be used, but it is easier to use and apply a second coat of quick-drying nontoxic latex. Paint adhesion is very important here, so do check the compatibility of each product you choose.

I have given these tiles an irregular, multi-colored pattern, painting each tile a different color. The possibilities are endless, however—you could use these methods to paint any pattern you choose.

Planning your time

DAY ONE
AM: Fill cracks, clean grout, and sand down

PM: *Tile paint method—*Start painting with special tile paint. *Household paint method—*Apply tile primer

DAY TWO
AM: *Tile paint method—*Continue painting with special tile paint; apply a second coat. *Household paint method—*Start painting on top of tile primer

PM: *Household paint method—*Apply second coat of paint on top of tile primer

Tools and materials

Sandpaper

Special tile paint (if applicable)

Tile primer (if using household paint)

Latex paint (if using household paint)

Household paintbrush

Small flat brush for edges and corners

Grout cleaner, scrubbing brush, and cloth

Tile spackle

Putty knife

Tough floor sealer (if using household paint)

1

2

3

Tile paint method

Day One

Step 1
Fill and repair cracks with tough floor tile spackle, and when it is dry, sand it down to a smooth, even finish.

Step 2
If you are not going to paint over the whole surface, but paint each tile separately, use a grout cleaner. Scrub it on with a brush, then wipe it off.

Step 3
Sand the floor with a fine-grit paper. On old tiles, the glaze will have worn away naturally. The areas to rub more are those that have not had much wear.

Step 4
Experiment with colors, mixing paints of the same kind in small quantities.

4

Step 5
Apply special tile paint with a normal household brush.

Step 6
Use a thin, flat brush for the corners and edges of the tiles. Apply a second coat of paint the following day if required and allow to dry for as long as you can before walking on it.

Household paint method

Day One

Step 1
Fill and repair cracks with tile spackle, and allow to dry. Sand this down to a smooth, even finish. This method requires tile primer, and since more coats of paint are required, I painted over the whole floor, including the grout. Allow this to dry fully overnight.

Day Two

Step 2
Apply the paint of your choice. Allow to dry before applying a second coat. The following evening, seal the paint with two coats of tough floor sealer.

Decorating ideas
You can create all kinds of patterns with the paint you apply—you could make a small stencil or paint a small motif by hand.

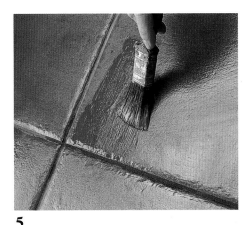
5

6

1

2

Old oak woodgraining

Damaged floorboards or those that have already been painted are difficult to renovate. Simply paint them to look like an aged and mellowed oak floor.

Y ou may be forgiven for at first wondering, "why paint wood to look like wood?" Well, perhaps your floorboards are beyond repair—they have been repaired too often and are too damaged to renovate to a good wooden finish, leaving paint as the only option. Or perhaps they have been painted already and rather than stripping them down completely it is easier to repaint them. Or maybe you prefer the look of a beautiful old oak floor.

Woodgraining can be a very specialized art practiced by master craftspeople to the highest exactitude, but do not worry. This project will not involve training to become an expert woodgrainer! Instead, I shall explain an easy, yet effective, technique to simulate a simple oak grain.

This method for woodgraining is an enjoyable and relaxing effect to paint, and lets you concentrate on the beautiful character of natural wood. It is helpful to look at veneer samples of various grains, and to take photographs when you see interesting old oak gates, doors, and floors. The more wood you look at, the easier it becomes to develop a feel for the flow and beautiful structure of natural grain and figuring.

On the evening before you start this project, prepare the floor by applying a coat or two of acrylic eggshell paint.

Day One

Step 1

Fill in holes and knots in the floorboards. If the wood is bare remember to seal any knots, sand down for a smooth surface, and prime it.

Step 2

Prepare the floor by applying a base coat of sand-colored acrylic eggshell paint. You may have to apply two coats if you are painting over an absorbent primer. If the surface is already painted, sand it down to provide a key, or rough surface, for the new paint to adhere to. Remember to paint in the direction of the woodgrain, and allow to dry thoroughly.

Step 3

Prepare a colored glaze. Pour some glaze into a bucket and slowly add acrylic colorizer. I used a ready-mixed colorizer, the color of medium oak.

Step 4

Paint on the glaze in the direction of the grain. Paint the length of two or three boards at a time.

Step 5

Add a dab of burnt umber acrylic paint directly from the tube onto the tip of your brush.

1

2

3

4

5

6

7

8

Step 6

Paint the color on the tip of your brush into the glaze, blending it in.

Step 7

Pull a metal decorator's comb through the glaze in one direction.

Step 8

Drag the comb a second time over the glaze, but this time at an angle to produce a mottled effect in the grain. Work fairly quickly on this before the glaze starts to dry. If the comb lines are too hard in places, soften them lightly with a brush.

Day Two

Step 9

When the mottled base is dry, paint on the quartered figuring. Do this by diluting a little burnt umber acrylic paint and apply it with a small, thin brush. It is always helpful to look at a piece of real oak as reference for how the figuring is formed.

Step 10

Soften the figuring, working gently with a soft brush in an outward direction.

Step 11

Add sharper, straighter marks across the grain to complete the figuring. When it's completely dry, varnish the floor with two coats of a tough floor sealer.

9

10

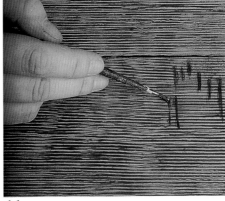

11

Fake leopard rug

An imitation leopard skin rug allows the beauty of this print-like pattern to be admired without cruelty. This is fun to paint and will add a touch of the exotic to any room.

Beautiful animal skin patterns are often simulated in fabric and fake fur, and this project is meant to result in a fun paint technique rather than a dead leopard!

To enhance the colors in the leopard skin I painted a base of strong deep-red acrylic eggshell paint. I drew the leopard-skin outline over the base in an appropriate place on the floor and then painted it in.

You could take the same technique further and paint a tiger, giraffe, or cheetah print in the same way.

The effect here was painted on floorboards, but you could paint this on almost any surface that the base coat is suitable for. If you want to prepare a new base coat color such as the deep red I used, apply eggshell paint the evening before you start the project—or you could paint directly over your existing floor color. Either way, your Sunday afternoon for this weekend will be completely free—for lounging about and eating grapes.

Planning your time

DAY ONE
AM: Draw outline of leopard shape and apply base coat

PM: Paint on leopard pattern print

DAY TWO
AM: Seal with acrylic varnish; allow to dry for an hour or so, then paint on a coat of oil-based varnish adding oil color to shade

PM: Apply final oil-based clear varnish

Tools and materials

Base coat of acrylic eggshell paint and roller or brush to apply this

Acrylic eggshell paint (sand color) as base coat for the leopard

Burnt umber and black poster color

Acrylic floor varnish

Oil-based varnish

Household paintbrush

Small brush to paint leopard print

Flogging (or long-bristled) brush to create fur flecks

Artist's oil paint to color oil-based varnish

Lacquer thinner

Day One

Step 1

Draw the outline of the rug with a piece of chalk.

1

2

Step 2

Paint within the outline of the shape with latex satin or acrylic eggshell paint (I used a sand color). Paint this base color in an outward direction in a "V" shape from the center of the leopard, exaggerating the brush strokes to accentuate the direction on the pattern.

Step 3

Mix a brown water-based glaze. I used burnt umber poster color, diluted with water, and a dollop of acrylic glaze.

Step 4

Once the base color is completely dry, apply the glaze with a brush, following the direction of the base color. If the glaze does not stick to the surface, wipe it off and reapply it—this should cure the surface and the glaze should adhere a second time.

3

Step 5

Immediately afterward, flog this to create a flecked pattern, again following the "V"-shaped direction; a flogging brush is ideal for this technique. With a tapping motion, flog along the "V" shape, breaking up the color and creating a flecked, hair-like effect.

Flogging

If you do not have a flogging brush, you could use a long-bristled dragging brush to create the flecked hair-like pattern.

4

5

Step 6

You will have to glaze over the outline to achieve an even finish, so wipe this off with a damp cloth as soon as possible.

Step 7

Mix a dark brown poster color of thick, opaque consistency (I used burnt umber mixed with black). Once the flecked effect has completely dried, apply the leopard spots, starting in the middle of the rug.

Step 8

Work the pattern outward, following the "V" shape, and mirroring the pattern on each side of the center. Allow this to dry overnight.

Day Two

Step 9

To seal the leopard rug, apply a coat of acylic varnish. Make sure the base is completely dry, otherwise this water-based varnish will pull off the paint.

Allow to dry for an hour or so. When dry, apply an oil-based varnish on top of this, but this time dab the brush with a touch of burnt umber oil paint. Work this into the center of the rug, leaving clear varnish on the edges.

Step 10

If you want to, paint a black line around the rug to simulate a black felt underlay. When completely dry, apply a final varnish. I used an oil-based varnish and added a hint of burnt umber oil paint to shade the pattern further.

Using lacquer thinner

When wiping off oil-based varnish and oil paint remember that you need to use a little lacquer thinner on your cloth. Afterward, clean the brushes with lacquer thinner, then with soapy water.

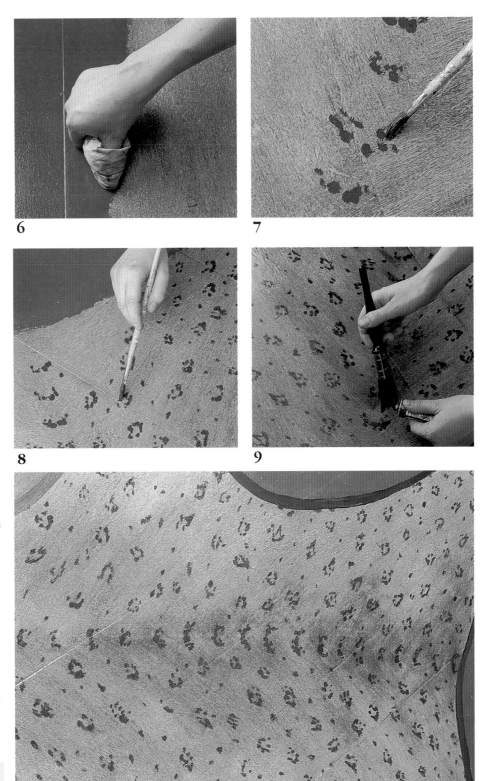

6

7

8

9

10

Simple mosaic floor

Here is a quick and effective way of creating a beautiful mosaic floor. A full spectrum of colors gives the potential for a wealth of motifs and interesting patterns.

T he small glass tiles used here are those usually found at the bottom of a swimming pool. They are available in a wide range of colors—even in gold and silver leaf.

It is a good idea to buy some sample pieces first and to look at the colors at home—it is amazing how different a color can appear away from artificial store lighting. I found that having a handful of sample tiles at home is the best way to experiment with color combinations and patterns.

Use tile nippers to cut the outside tiles or those that fit around any obstacles, such as a sink pedestal. The tiles can be cut to any shape and made to create every kind of motif—but complicated projects take much longer than a weekend, so prior planning and thought are essential! A simple pattern like this one, though, can easily be accomplished within two days and even leave plenty of time for thinking about the next mosaic idea!

Some time before you start on this project, calculate how many tiles are required and buy sheets of tiles and other materials.

Planning your time

DAY ONE
AM: Lay out the blue sheets and design your pattern; pull out blue tiles where white ones are to go

PM: Apply adhesive to the floor and lay the tiles

DAY TWO
AM: Glue down any loose tiles with strong fast-drying glue, then apply grout

Tools and materials

Glass mosaic swimming-pool tiles

Tile adhesive and notched trowel

Fast-drying glue

Floor grout

Craft knife

Tile nippers (if you need to cut the outer tiles)

Cloth

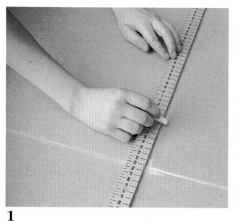

1

2

3

Day One

Step 1

Measure the floor to approximate how many tiles you require. They are usually available in sheets of 250. Mark the center point of the floor and start the design from this point.

Step 2

Soak the sheets of white tiles (those to be placed onto the blue background) in water. The paper backing will slip off.

Step 3

Lay out the sheets of blue tiles and mark out the pattern with the white tiles on top. This is a good way to plan your design; rearrange it until you are happy with it.

Step 4

Use tile cutters if you have to cut tiles to fit the edge of the floor or to fit around an obstacle.

Step 5

With a craft knife, lift out the squares of blue that are to be replaced with the white pattern.

Step 6

Using a notched trowel, apply a thin coating of tile adhesive to the surface. Work in small areas at a time, applying enough adhesive for one sheet of tiles. This will ensure that the adhesive stays wet and the tiles stick down well.

4

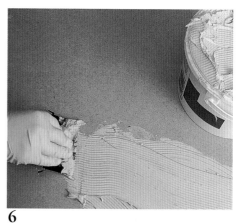

5

6

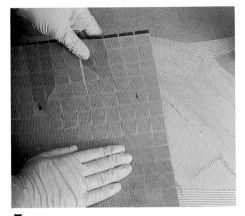

7

Step 7

Lay the blue sheets down in place, pressing them firmly into the adhesive.

Step 8

Tear back the brown paper where the holes have been made to insert the loose white tiles.

Step 9

Insert the white tiles. I also inserted some mirrored tiles.

Day Two

Step 10

When the adhesive is dry, wash off the brown paper that still remains on the blue tiles. Wet the paper and it will just peel or wash off.

Run your fingers over the tiles and check to see if they have all stuck well to the adhesive. Any loose tiles should be lifted off and stuck down with strong glue.

Step 11

Apply grout. I used a standard gray floor-tile grout, following the manufacturer's instructions.

Step 12

Wipe off the grout with a slightly damp clean cloth, changing to another clean cloth to finish.

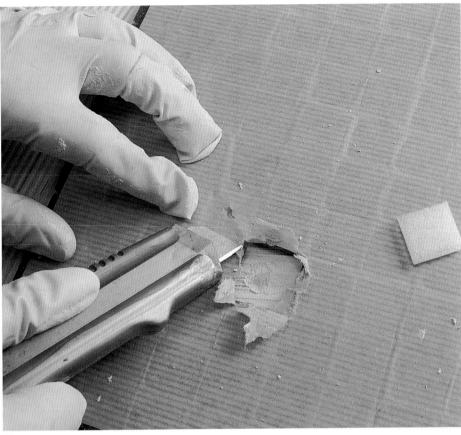

8

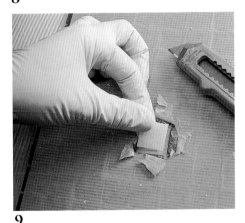

9

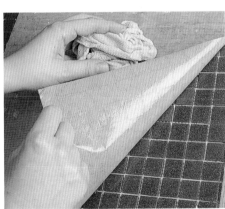

10

11

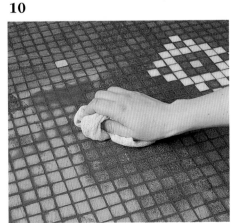

12

Painted stair runner

This brightly colored stair runner has been achieved with acrylic paint and is extremely practical. Cut to fit a staircase, it can be taken up when you move.

This stair runner is made of a canvas cloth cut to size and then primed, painted, and sealed. Runners were often used in the eighteenth century and are now becoming popular again. Like rugs, they are not permanently fixed to the floor, so you can take them with you when you move and can even repaint them. Also, since they have a varnished finish, they are not only durable, but wipeable too.

Runners can be given all manner of decorative ideas, styles, and colors. I sealed this runner with a light, flexible gel, and then applied artist's acrylic colors. These colors tend to be purer and stronger than decorator's latex-based paints. Since they are applied to a sealed surface, only a little color is needed.

The runner shown here was cut to fit the width and length of the stairs and then held in place with standard stair rods. The runner can be cut to any shape and size—you could even make one great big one to fit an entire room.

Planning your time

DAY ONE
AM: Measure and cut canvas, and prime with acrylic soft gel medium

PM: Paint green base coat

DAY TWO
AM: Paint flowers

PM: Finish painting flowers and dots; finally, varnish with top coat varnish, and once dry, apply a second coat

Tools and materials

18oz (500g) cotton duck canvas

Acrylic soft gel medium

Acrylic paints

Top coat varnish

Tailor's chalk

Scissors

Fabric glue

Bucket

Household paintbrush

Thin brush for painting flowers and dots

Chalk

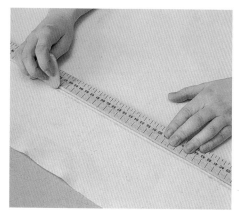

1

Day One

Step 1
Measure the size of runner required from 18oz (500g) cotton duck canvas and mark this with tailor's chalk.

Step 2
Cut the canvas, leaving about ¾" (2cm) all around to turn under as a hem later.

Step 3
Seal the canvas with two coats of acrylic soft gel, applying it with a paintbrush. Make sure you cover the canvas completely—any parts you miss will show up later and spoil the surface of the runner.

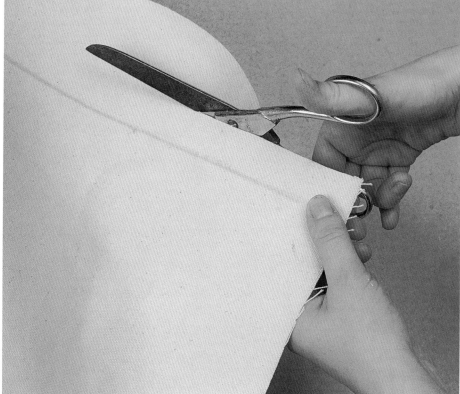

2

Getting rid of creases
If the runner is cut from the end of a roll of canvas and is creased, iron this out before painting it.

3

4

5

6

Step 4
Prepare the base color of diluted acrylic paint; I used a bright green. Squirt some acrylic paint into a bucket and slowly add water to dilute it.

Step 5
Apply the acrylic mix to the runner in a horizontal direction.

Step 6
Change the color slightly by adding different greens to the acrylic mix.

Step 7
Apply the new color, blending this in with your brush to achieve lighter and darker tones.

7

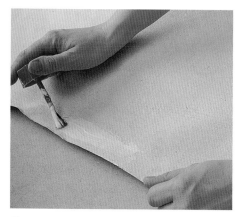

8

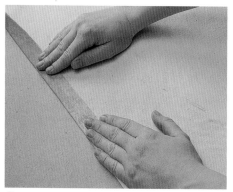

9

10

Step 8
Once this base color is dry, apply fabric glue along the back edges of the runner.

Step 9
Firmly stick down the edges.

Day Two

Step 10
Plan the top design, drawing circular flower shapes with chalk dots.

Step 11
With a thin brush, join these dots and fill in the shapes with paint to form the petals of flowers.

11

Step 12
Go over the flowers with a slightly different color to give more definition.

Step 13
Paint the center circles of the flowers.

Step 14
Once all the flowers are complete, add other dots and lines to balance the overall pattern.

Step 15
Once dry, apply two coats of acrylic top coat varnish, allowing it to dry between each coat.

12

13

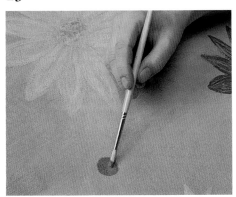

14

15

Staple gun and mallet

Transfer paper

Wax filler sticks

Rollers
Use paint rollers and trays for preparing and varnishing floors quickly. Rinse new rollers first to keep the hairs from coming out into the paint.

Sanding sealer
Used to seal wood before final varnishing, or before opening the grain and liming.

Shellac
Solution applied to seal knots in wood and keep resin from seeping through. Not necessary for old wood that has fully dried out or for new wood that has been thoroughly kiln dried.

Softening brush
Special brush with very soft bristles used for gently brushing over paint and glaze work either to blend or slightly blurr and generally soften its effect.

Spray adhesive
Spray-on, low-tack glue used for holding stencils in place and repositioning them.

Staple gun and mallet
Used to staple down sheets of hardboard onto the floor.

Stencil brushes
Small round brushes with a flat top used for stenciling. The brushes with very flat tops are best used for rubbing on cream-like stencil paint.

Tack cloth
Thin sticky cloth bought in sealed packet used to clean off final dust before painting or varnishing.

Tailor's chalk
Colored chalk used to mark fabric. It can be brushed off.

Tile adhesive
Can be bought pre-mixed in a paste. For sticking tiles onto the floor before grouting, apply with a notched trowel.

Tile primer
White primer for ceramic tiles. It dries overnight.

Top coat varnish
Flexible varnish used for stair runners. Dries to a gloss finish.

Transfer paper
Used like carbon paper to draw over and so transfer designs.

Wax filler sticks
Sticks of colored wax used to fill in small holes in floorboards.

Wood stain
Prepared colors available in a water and solvent base to color wood. Stain seeps right into the grain of the wood.

Suppliers

GENERAL CRAFT

Hobby Lobby
7707 SW 44th Street
Oklahoma City, OK 73179
Tel: (405) 745-1100
www.hobbylobby.com

Michaels Arts & Crafts
8000 Bent Branch Drive
Irving, TX 75063
Tel: (214) 409-1300
www.michaels.com

Zim's Crafts, Inc.
4370 South 300 West
Salt Lake City, UT 84107
Toll free: (800) 453-6420
Tel: (801) 268-2505
Fax: (801) 268-9859
www.zimscrafts.com

GENERAL ART SUPPLIES

Jo-Ann Fabrics and Crafts
www.joann.com
(website includes store locator)
Store questions: (888) 739-4120

HARDWARE/
HOME IMPROVEMENT STORES

Home Depot U.S.A., Inc.
2455 Paces Ferry Road
Atlanta, GA 30339-4024
Tel: (770) 433-8211
www.homedepot.com

Lowe's Home Improvement Warehouse
Customer Care (ICS7)

Lowe's Companies, Inc.
P.O. Box 1111
North Wilkesboro, NC 28656
Toll free: (800) 44-LOWES
www.lowes.com

PAINT PRODUCTS

Delta Technical Coatings
2550 Pellissier Place
Whittier, CA 90601
Toll free: (800) 423-4135
Fax: (562) 695-5157
www.deltacrafts.com
Acrylic, glass, and fabric paints.

EK Success
P.O. Box 1141
Clifton, NJ 07014-1141
Toll free: (800) 524-1349
success@eksuccess.com
www.eksuccess.com
Paints and general craft products.

Pébéo of America
P.O. Box 714
Route 78, Airport Rd.
Swanton, VT 05488
Toll free: (800) 363-5012
Fax: (819) 821-4151
Glass paints, markers, and mediums.

Liquitex-Binney and Smith
P.O. Box 431
Easton, PA 18044-0431
Tel: (888) 422-7954
www.liquitex.com
Paints, mediums, varnishes, and additives.

PAINTBRUSHES

Loew-Cornell
563 Chestnut Ave.
Teaneck, NJ 07666-2490
Tel: (201) 836-7070
Fax: (201) 836-8110
www.loew-cornell.com

FABRIC CRAFTS/NOTIONS

Coats & Clark
P.O. Box 27067
Greenville, NC 29616
Toll free: (800) 648-1479
www.coatsandclark.com
General purpose threads.

Dharma Trading Co.
P.O. Box 150916
San Rafael, CA 94915
Toll free: (800) 542-5227
catalog@dharmatrading.com
www.dharmatrading.com
Fabric dyes, paints, and fabric art products.

STENCILS

American Traditional Stencils
442 First New Hampshire Turnpike
Northwood, NH 03261-3401
Tel: (603) 942-8100
www.americantraditional.com

Royal Design Studio
2504 Transportation Ave., Suite H
National City, CA 91950
Toll free: (800) 747-9767
www.royaldesignstudio.com

Index